WEAPON

THE LUGER

NEIL GRANT

Series Editor Martin Pegler
Illustrated by Johnny Shumate & Alan Gilliland

OSPREY PUBLISHING
Bloomsbury Publishing Plc

Kemp House, Chawley Park, Oxford OX2 9PH, UK
29 Earlsfort Terrace, Dublin 2, Ireland
1385 Broadway, 5th Floor, New York, NY 10018, USA
Email: info@ospreypublishing.com
www.ospreypublishing.com

OSPREY is a trademark of Osprey Publishing Ltd

First published in Great Britain in 2018

© Osprey Publishing Ltd, 2018

Transferred to digital in 2022

A catalogue record for this book is available from the
British Library.

Print ISBN: 978 1 4728 1973 4
ePub: 978 1 4728 1975 8
ePDF: 978 1 4728 1974 1
XML: 978 1 4728 2333 5

Index by Rob Munro
Typeset by PDQ Digital Media Solutions, Bungay, UK
Printed and bound in India by Replika Press Private Ltd.

24 25 26 27 28   10 9 8 7 6 5 4

The Woodland Trust
Osprey Publishing supports the Woodland Trust, the UK's leading
woodland conservation charity.

www.ospreypublishing.com
To find out more about our authors and books visit our website.
Here you will find extracts, author interviews, details of
forthcoming events and the option to sign-up for our newsletter.

Dedication
For Charlie McKeown, Weapons Collection Manager at the
Small Arms School Corps, for his help with this and other books.

Acknowledgements
With thanks to the Small Arms School Collection at Warminster,
Ian McCollum, Mike Cooper, Jonathan Ferguson, Range Days in
France, Jérôme Giolat, Douglas de Souza Aguiar Jr, Rostand
Medeiros and Filipe do Amaral Monteiro. Photographs not
otherwise credited are from the author's collection.

Editor's note
Metric measurements are used in this book. For ease of
comparison please refer to the following conversion table:

1m = 1.09yd / 3.28ft / 39.37in
1cm = 0.39in
1mm = 0.04in
1kg = 2.20lb
1g = 0.04oz

The Royal Armouries
The Royal Armouries is Britain's national museum of arms and
armour, and one of the most important museums of its type in
the world. Its origins lie in the Middle Ages, and at its core is the
celebrated collection originating in the nation's working arsenal,
assembled over many centuries at the Tower of London. In the
reign of Elizabeth I, selected items began to be arranged for
display to visitors, making the Royal Armouries heir to one of
the oldest deliberately created visitor attractions in the country.
The collection is now housed and displayed at three sites: the
White Tower at the Tower of London, a purpose-built museum in
Leeds, and Fort Nelson near Portsmouth. To find out more,
explore online at collections.royalarmouries.org

Front cover, above: A Pistole 08 in the Small Arms School
Collection. The P 08 was the most common of the Luger models
by a significant margin.
Front cover, below: A Soviet officer tries out one of the countless
thousands of Lugers captured on the Eastern Front during World
War II. Captured Lugers were popular souvenirs, whether or not
their new owners planned to use them in anger. (Herbert
Hoffmann/ullstein bild via Getty Images)
Title page: Though short-ranged compared to a rifle, the Luger's
compactness and rapid fire made it a useful weapon for house
clearing, as shown here after the German capture of Sevastopol,
Crimea, in July 1942. (Keystone/Getty Images)

CONTENTS

INTRODUCTION

The Luger is among the most famous 20th-century pistols. Its distinctive appearance has been immortalized in countless war movies and books, but its importance goes well beyond this. It evolved from the Borchardt, the first true semi-automatic pistol and the first weapon with a detachable box magazine. It dominated the semi-automatic pistol market for the first decades of the 20th century, and was adopted by countries from Bulgaria to Chile and from Norway to Persia. It is most famous, though, as the German military pistol through both world wars. Captured examples became popular souvenirs and many British servicemen in both wars preferred it to their issue pistols. It soldiered on in unexpected places after World War II, with French soldiers in Indochina and Algeria, and both Portuguese troops and communist-backed guerrillas in Africa in the 1960s. The final examples remained in Norwegian service until the 1980s. The Luger's iconic status saw it return to production in the 1970s, for sale in the collector's market.

Tactically, long-barrelled versions served as early submachine-gun equivalents in the trench fighting of World War I, equipped with shoulder stocks and high-capacity drum magazines. Technically, the Luger family spawned two of the most prolific military pistol cartridges of the century, used in almost every Western and Soviet submachine gun.

The Luger story is full of unexpected quirks. The weapon is usually regarded as a quintessentially German pistol, but was actually first adopted by the Swiss, and considered as a potential service pistol by both Britain and the USA. Its users would rarely have called it a 'Luger'. It was the Pistole 08 (P 08) to German soldiers, while its manufacturer called it the 'Parabellum', from the Latin *Si vis pacem, para bellum* ('If you want peace, prepare for war') which formed the company motto and telegraphic address. The Luger name was actually popularized by the US importer, and the pistols produced in the 1970s could not legally be called 'Lugers' in the United States, as the importer still held that trademark and was

4

The Luger was the main pistol of the German armed forces for 40 years, in three main variants: the Pistole 08 (**1**) with 100mm barrel and fixed sights; the Navy's Pistole 04 (**2**) with 150mm barrel and two-position rear sights; and the Lange Pistole 08 (**3**) with 200mm barrel and sights adjustable to 800m. These examples are from the Small Arms School Collection.

using it to sell pistols of their own design. This book uses 'Luger' rather than the more strictly correct 'Parabellum', however, as the former is more familiar to English-speaking readers.

The Luger has spawned a significant literature, and a book of this length can only be an introduction. It focuses on the technical development of the pistol and its practical use in combat, rather than on proof marks and manufacturer codes, beloved of collectors but with little practical effect. Its primary emphasis is placed upon German Lugers, which formed the majority of production, but it does discuss significant foreign users. It cannot cover every detail or variation, but those seeking more information will find further sources in the Bibliography.

Two soldiers with P 08s and stick grenades storm out of a bunker on the Western Front, 1939. The picture is part of a long series of posed propaganda photos in which the photographer made the men rush out of the door over and over until he was satisfied with the result. The man on the right has improvised a lanyard for his pistol. (Bundesarchiv, Bild 101I-048-1119-26 / photo: Schweizer)

DEVELOPMENT
The first semi-automatic pistols

ORIGINS

The Luger's immediate ancestor – the Borchardt C93 – was the first semi-automatic pistol to enter production, but numerous other semi-automatics arrived shortly afterwards. These competing designs all appeared at the end of the 19th century due to radical innovation in firearms technology over the previous 50 years.

Typical military pistols in 1840 were single-shot black-powder weapons firing large-calibre lead balls, essentially unchanged from the Napoleonic period. Most were smoothbore muzzle-loaders. The accuracy advantages of rifling were well understood, but loading a ball down the grooves of a rifled barrel took much longer than a smoothbore, and because pistols were short-ranged weapons, the extra cost was rarely seen as worthwhile. Percussion caps – thin metal cases containing fulminate of mercury which detonated when struck – had been available for some time, but were now entering general military use. Initially, they simply replaced the flint in a conventional flintlock pistol – indeed, many existing flintlocks were converted to use caps instead. The caps reduced the frequency of misfires – often around 10 per cent with flintlocks – and improved accuracy by reducing the delay (so-called 'lock time') between pulling the trigger and the weapon firing. The full potential of percussion caps was realized when the first practical revolvers appeared in the 1840s. These had cylinders with five or six chambers loaded with powder and ball and with nipples for percussion caps at the rear. A new chamber rotated into line with the barrel for firing each time the hammer was pulled back to cock the weapon.

The new revolvers had rifled barrels, because the charge was loaded into the cylinder directly rather than forced down the barrel, making them more accurate than the old pistols. They gave a single man unprecedented firepower, as their use in the American Civil War (1861–65) showed. Loading each chamber separately with powder, ball and percussion cap made reloading these cap-and-ball revolvers in action unfeasible, however. American cavalrymen often carried several pistols, but there were clearly practical limits to this.

The next improvement was to encase bullet, propellant and percussion cap in a brass cartridge. This had several advantages. First, the rigid metallic cartridge case protected its contents from moisture or damage, allowing cartridges to be held in magazines and withstand handling by the action of repeating weapons. Second, detonation of the propellant expanded the ductile brass case to fill the chamber completely, eliminating the gas-leakage problems that dogged early bolt-action rifles such as the Dreyse. Third, metallic cases prevented overheating as the brass case absorbed most of the heat from the propellant detonating, and expelled it with the spent case. Excessive chamber heating only really became a problem with fully automatic weapons, however, rather than pistols. Metallic cartridges allowed the creation of practical bolt- or lever-action repeaters such as the American Winchester and the German Mauser Gewehr 71/84, while some revolvers introduced swing-out cylinder or break-open designs that allowed faster, easier reloading.

One more improvement was required before semi-automatic pistols became practical weapons. Early metallic cartridges were still loaded with conventional 'black powder'. This was a 'low explosive' of limited power, which produced large amounts of smoke and carbon fouling when fired. This high level of fouling was tolerable – if undesirable – in revolvers, as their actions were manually operated by the firer, and were thus relatively robust. By contrast, a semi-automatic pistol's more sensitive action quickly became unreliable as fouling built up. The answer came in 1884, when French chemist Paul Vieille invented the first successful smokeless powder. Called *poudre blanche* or 'white powder', to distinguish it from standard 'black powder', this was a stabilized form of the high-explosive

The 10.6mm black-powder Reichsrevolver 79 (above) and Reichsrevolver 83 (below) were old-fashioned even when adopted, but shortage of more modern weapons would keep them in service with Germany's artillery and rear-echelon troops until the end of World War I.

nitrocellulose. It produced almost three times more power than the same weight of black powder, would burn when wet, and produced little smoke and far less fouling. This cleaner-burning smokeless powder made semi-automatic pistols viable. Its greater power also allowed a change from traditional large-calibre pistol balls, fired at relatively low velocity, to smaller bullets fired at much higher velocity. Higher velocity meant a flatter trajectory, because the shorter flight time to the target meant gravity had less time to act on the bullet, and thus better range and accuracy. Because less of Vieille's powder was needed to deliver the same energy, the new cartridges could be significantly shorter than their black-powder predecessors. This made putting a magazine in the grip of a pistol possible, though designers were surprisingly slow to take advantage of this.

Smokeless powder made semi-automatic pistols possible, but they still had to be created. The simplest design used expanding propellant gas from the fired cartridge to drive an unlocked breechblock rearwards, compressing a return spring. The spent cartridge was ejected as the breechblock reached the limit of rearward travel. The compressed return spring then sent the breechblock forward again, stripping the next round off the magazine and chambering it. The breechblock's rearward travel had to take long enough to ensure the bullet left the muzzle before the spent cartridge was ejected, or high-pressure propellant gas trapped in the barrel behind the bullet would vent through the ejection port, endangering the firer. More powerful cartridges pushed the breechblock back faster, while using heavier breechblocks or stronger springs slowed the action down again. Limits on how heavy a pistol breechblock could be, and how powerful a return spring it could use, meant this 'simple blowback' mechanism was only suitable for pocket pistols firing low-powered cartridges, however. More powerful military pistol rounds needed locking mechanisms to keep the breech closed until pressure dropped to safe levels, but then unlock the action for the residual pressure to eject the spent case and load a new round.

THE BORCHARDT C93

The first successful semi-automatic pistol design was created by Hugo Borchardt, who was born in Saxony in 1844, but emigrated to the United States as a young man, becoming a naturalized US citizen. Borchardt gained considerable experience of firearms design in the United States, working for Colt and later Winchester and Sharps. He designed several revolver prototypes for Winchester in 1876–77, which survive in the company's museum. Unfortunately, Winchester seems to have regarded its pistol designs as bargaining chips to keep Colt out of the repeating rifle market – while Colt did not make rifles, Winchester would not make pistols. Borchardt's revolver designs were thus never exploited. Whether or not Borchardt was disappointed by this, he was back in Europe by 1881, though he returned to the United States later as a consultant to Remington. More importantly, in 1893 he designed a pistol for the German arms manufacturer Ludwig Loewe & Co.

The Borchardt pistol used a toggle-locked breech. This had a two-piece linkage, hinged in the middle like a knee joint, and attached to the rear of the breechblock. Although it required high-quality machining, the toggle lock was both strong and reliable, and easily able to handle powerful rounds.

The Borchardt pistol also fed from a detachable box magazine in the pistol grip. This seems an obvious design today, but was revolutionary at the time. Putting the magazine into the grip rather than ahead of it shortened the weapon by several centimetres, improved the balance of the pistol, and – because one hand will always find the other – it made reloading more intuitive in poor light. Despite this, most other designers continued to place pistol magazines ahead of the grip for some time. Other early semi-automatics were charger loaded, requiring the firer to place a charger of rounds into a guide above the open breech and slide the rounds down into a fixed internal magazine, as with a bolt-action rifle. Using box magazines allowed faster reloading and gave better protection to the rounds. Again, however, detachable magazines did not become standard on other pistols until a decade later.

Revolver rounds used a rim around the cartridge base to locate themselves in the cylinder, but did not feed well in a box magazine. The Borchardt used a 7.65×25mm bottleneck cartridge case, with a groove around the base creating a 'rim' for the extractor to grip without protruding past the sides of the case itself. This cartridge – designed by Georg Luger – would ultimately prove to be as influential as the pistol itself.

Borchardt supplied his pistol with a wooden shoulder stock which attached to the rear of the frame, turning the weapon into a semi-automatic carbine. Response to the new weapon was very positive. The *Boston Herald* newspaper of 22 November 1894 noted 'The naval small arms board had exhibited before it today a pistol which is quite likely to revolutionize this sort of equipment in the armies and navies of the world'. The Borchardt had problems, however. It used a clock-type mainspring, which required a large housing protruding far behind the grip. The spring also needed to be carefully balanced to the cartridge used, and could function erratically with different batches of ammunition. The grip was set awkwardly at right angles to the barrel, leading to poor pointability. Overall, the pistol was long, heavy and poorly balanced. More importantly, the mechanism was complex and difficult to strip and

This Borchardt from the Small Arms School Collection is shown with its wooden stock and attached holster. Note the vertical grip angle and large rear overhang. When the pistol fired, the two pieces of the toggle were in a straight line, and both barrel and toggle initially moved backwards together. At a set distance, an internal roller caused the hinge joint to break upwards, pulling the breechblock away from the rear of the barrel and ejecting the spent case. The spring then sent the breechblock forward again, chambering the next round. The system resembled that of the well-proven Maxim machine gun, except that the Maxim toggle breaks downwards into the body of the gun. Because the pistol lacked sufficient internal space for this to occur, Borchardt inverted the mechanism to break upwards.

reassemble for maintenance even in ideal conditions, let alone in the field. In consequence, while Borchardt's pistol attracted much interest, no army seriously considered adopting it. The exact number produced is unknown, but the highest known serial number is 3013, so fewer than 3,500 seems likely.

THE BORCHARDT-LUGER

The Borchardt C93 was the first viable semi-automatic pistol, but it was quickly joined by others of varying quality. Most notably, the Mauser C96 'Broomhandle' appeared shortly after, also chambered for the Luger-developed Borchardt cartridge but with a more powerful propellant loading. The C96 had a rifle-style charger-loaded fixed magazine ahead of the grip, but it was a well-made gun, although early versions had reliability problems, and it benefited from Mauser's strong reputation. The Borchardt needed improvement to remain competitive, but Borchardt was apparently reluctant to do so. Possibly he felt it was already perfect, or he did not understand practical battlefield realities. He may simply have been working on other projects, being involved with designing gas-heating and -lighting appliances at the time.

Ludwig Loewe & Co had merged with several other arms firms to create Deutsche Waffen- und Munitionsfabriken ('German Weapons and Ammunition Factories', or DWM) which asked Georg Luger – who designed the Borchardt's cartridge – to improve the pistol. A former Austrian Army officer and an excellent marksman, Luger spoke several languages fluently. He joined Ludwig Loewe & Co in 1891 as both an engineer and a salesman, demonstrating products to potential customers. These experiences gave him a more practical understanding of what was required of service weapons, and he was improving an existing product, rather than starting from scratch. These improvements were made at different stages during the Swiss pistol trials outlined below, but are drawn together here for clarity.

The clock-type mainspring was an obvious weak point. Luger replaced it with a leaf-type mainspring, placed in the back of the grip. This did away with the complex and troublesome adjustments previously required and simplified maintenance. It also removed the large rear overhang, reducing the Borchardt's length and weight while improving balance. The internal roller to break the toggle lock was replaced by ramps machined into the exterior of the frame, a much simpler and stronger design. When the toggle drums hit these ramps, they automatically cammed upwards, breaking the toggle joint. Luger shortened his original 7.65×25mm ammunition design to 7.65×21mm, creating the 7.65mm Parabellum cartridge. Because the pistol's action must take the round at least its own length to the rear to eject it, a shorter round meant a shorter action, thus reducing overall length. The shorter rounds also allowed Luger to accommodate the new spring in the grip and still change the vertical grip of the Borchardt to one raked backward at 55 degrees, an ideal angle for natural pointability.

10

SWISS TRIALS

In June 1897, the Swiss military began trials to find a new self-loading service pistol. The Swiss had tested the Bergmann 1894 and Mannlicher 1894 in 1895 and it was felt nothing would be gained by testing them again, so only the Borchardt C93 and Mauser C96 were tested. The pistol currently in Swiss service, the 7.5mm Ordonnanzrevolver 1882, was to act as a control benchmark, but would not itself be tested. Georg Luger demonstrated the Borchardt C93, impressing the committee with its powerful high-velocity cartridge. Even so, the Borchardt C93's excessive size and poor balance meant it was not considered suitable to replace the issue revolver. Fitted with its shoulder stock, the Borchardt C93 was considered as a possible light carbine for the cavalry, but was let down by its complexity and (again) its poor balance. The Mauser C96 was similarly felt to be too big and complex.

After these trials results, DWM submitted an 'improved' Borchardt, with the recoil spring now located in the grip. This was tried against the Bergmann and Mannlicher in October 1897, but despite notable reductions in size and weight, it was still considered too big and too heavy. The Swiss scheduled new trials for October 1898, before a larger panel. Six pistols were submitted – the Bergmann 1897 (with locked breech) and 1898 (with unlocked breech), the Mannlicher 1897, the Roth, an improved Mauser C96 and an improved Borchardt pistol. Importantly, the Swiss agreed to DWM's request to replace the company's entry with a pair of 'Borchardt-Lugers' chambered for 7.65mm Parabellum in November 1898, before firing trials started. One of the Borchardt-Lugers was fitted with a long barrel, the other with a short barrel, and they were accompanied by a detachable 'holster-stock'.

The firing trials consisted of two rapid-fire tests (50 rounds each), an accuracy test (50 rounds at 50m), an endurance test (400 rounds in succession, without cleaning) and water and dust tests. The Borchardt-Lugers suffered very few jams or misfires, and were the most accurate of the guns submitted for the trials. The commission reported very positively, believing that the Borchardt-Lugers were undoubtedly the best of those pistols tested. The commission's second preference was the Mannlicher, although it had technically scored third, behind the Roth. Both of these pistols lost marks due to being charger loaded, while the Mannlicher's magazine was positioned ahead of the trigger rather than in the grip, and the Roth's safety features were deemed inadequate. The Bergmann pistols and the Mauser C96 failed to meet the minimum standards during the trials, and were eliminated.

A final round of trials was scheduled for May 1899, with a prize of 5,000 Swiss francs for the winning inventor. DWM submitted a pair of improved Borchardt-Lugers, in two barrel lengths. They were fitted with manual safety catches in addition to an improved grip safety, as suggested by the previous commission. The breechblocks were redesigned for smoother operation, and lightening cuts were machined into the frame to reduce weight. These pistols were easily superior to an improved Mannlicher also in the trials, while the Roth and Mauser weapons were excluded from further testing as they had not been improved since the previous trials.

The 'New Model' and short frame changes

The original Parabellum of 1900 (later dubbed the 'Old Model') was undoubtedly the best semi-automatic of its day, but still had problems. The breech closure was not always sufficiently positive, some small parts such as the thin spring-steel extractor were prone to breakage and there was no obvious way to tell whether a round was chambered or not. A revised 'New Model' appeared in 1906, with the more dependable coil mainspring replacing the original leaf-type mainspring to give more positive closure of the action, and a more robust extractor. The extractor protruded from the frame top when a cartridge was chambered, and had 'GELADEN' ('loaded') inscribed on the left side, acting as a visual and tactile indicator. The New Model also featured a wider trigger and flat toggle knobs (rather than those of the Old Model type, which were dished toward the rear), and omitted the anti-bounce lock from the right toggle grip. The latter supposedly prevented the breechblock bouncing back from the chamber face at the end of the return stroke in toggle-locked machine guns, but proved unnecessary with lighter pistol components. A new shorter frame (129mm versus 131mm) had been introduced a few years earlier. The long and short frames overlapped the change to the New Model and also to the new 9mm calibre becoming available. The small number of Old Model pistols produced in 9mm between that cartridge appearing in 1904 and the release of the 'New Model' in 1906 might have either frame, but most New Models have the short frame.

A pair of 'American Eagle' 7.65mm commercial pistols (see pages 70–71) showing differences between the 1900 'Old Model' (above) and the 1906 'New Model' (below). (© Royal Armouries PR.10774 and PR.4132)

leaving ten designs. Two revolvers from Colt and Smith & Wesson were rejected because they were very similar to the current issue weapons and the Board preferred the rate of fire and quicker loading of a self-loader. The Board found the Webley-Fosbery 'automatic revolver' (which used recoil energy to rotate the cylinder and recock itself after each shot) to be technically interesting but too heavy and complex, and as slow to reload as a revolver. The two semi-automatic pistols (one single-action, one double-action) submitted by US inventor William Knoble were rejected as being so crudely manufactured as to be unusable. Another semi-automatic design from a US inventor, the White-Merrill, was also rejected as inadequate and poorly developed. The Board did not favour the design of the Bergmann pistol – a modified M1906 – presumably because of its rather clumsy layout, with the magazine ahead of the trigger. Worse, the specially made ammunition sent with it was impounded by US Customs. The Bergmann proved incapable of firing standard US-supplied ammunition, suffering 13 misfires in 20 shots, apparently because its hammer strike was too weak to detonate the less sensitive US primers. This left three serious contenders – the Savage, the Luger and the Colt. The Savage was an unusual design locked by a rotating barrel. The committee liked its simplicity, but there was no automatic safety or loaded-chamber indicator and its grip (holding eight rounds rather than the seven held by the Colt and Luger designs) was uncomfortably thick. The Colt used John Browning's long-tested dropping-link design. It lacked

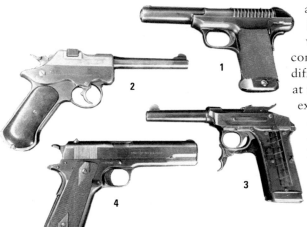

an automatic safety or loaded-chamber indicator and needed two hands to withdraw spent magazines, and the committee disliked its lateral ejection. It differed significantly from the later Colt 1911 at this point, with several features (such as an excessively vertical grip) that were rectified as a result of these trials. The Luger entry was a New Model-style prototype with a 127mm barrel, hand built because the .45-calibre (11.43mm) cartridge was too big to modify existing components to accept. The committee felt that the Luger's grip angle made shooting easy; they liked its vertical ejection, its loaded-chamber indicator and its automatic and manual safeties, but felt the breech closure was insufficiently positive.

Three of the competitors in the 1907 US pistol trials – the Savage 1907 (**1**), Knoble double-action (**2**) and White-Merrill (**3**) – and a Colt 1911 (**4**). The last-named pistol was not a competitor, but developed from the Colt entry. (Courtesy Forgotten Weapons)

All three pistols underwent rapid-fire, penetration and accuracy tests, followed by dust and rust tests. Unsurprisingly, the Luger was the most accurate of the pistols tested, and did well enough on the endurance tests, with most of the 14 stoppages in 641 rounds being due to the inconsistent government-supplied ammunition. Equally unsurprisingly, it did less well on the dust and rust tests, after which rounds had to be manually cycled through the action, though it functioned normally again after light external oiling. None of the three pistols was a clear winner, but the Colt had functioned somewhat more dependably than the others. The Board recommended awarding Colt and Savage contracts for 200 pistols each for large-scale testing, and that the Luger design not be taken forward. Savage declined the order, however, and the Board offered DWM a contract to produce 200 .45in Lugers for further testing against the Colt, at $48.75 each including two spare magazines and tools. After consideration, DWM also declined the order, and withdrew from the competition. After all, the US Army of the time was very small, and no-one could anticipate the vast expansion that would come during the two world wars. Moreover, it was clear from previous tests that the .45 Luger was unlikely to win, and the contract was being offered largely to provide a competitor for the Colt. Hand-building 200 pistols would be labour intensive and offered little profit, so DWM probably felt they would do better concentrating on the much larger German Army contract also on offer.

Savage later had a change of mind and accepted the contract for 200 further pistols, but neither these nor the Colt in its original form satisfied the Board, which suggested various improvements. The revised Colt design ultimately won, incorporating several features the Board had praised on the Luger, including the raked pistol grip and a grip safety.

It is often assumed that two .45-calibre Lugers were submitted for the US trials, based on an assumed surviving pistol being numbered '2', but the trial report itself refers only to one pistol. In fact, two .45 ACP Parabellums survive, and are often assumed to be pistols from the 1907 trial. The trials pistol was chambered for the .45 M1906 cartridge, though, not .45 ACP. Moreover, there are noticeable differences between these two pistols, and

UNUSUAL LUGERS

Luger carbines

Fitting pistols with shoulder stocks for increased range and accuracy was a common idea in the early 20th century; commercial Parabellums could

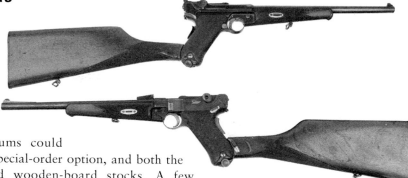

have stock lugs as a special-order option, and both the P 04 and LP 08 had wooden-board stocks. A few Parabellums were produced as true carbines, however. These had 300mm barrels with a chequered wooden forestock beneath, providing a grip for the left hand. The detachable wooden butts were fully rounded like rifle stocks, rather than the flat-board versions of the military pistol-carbines. Most were 7.65mm calibre and built on Old Model frames with grip safeties, though a few in 9mm and/or built on New Model frames exist.

A special high-powered cartridge was produced for these carbines, which not only made best use of the longer barrel, but also provided enough impetus to move the heavier barrel and working parts backwards, which the rather weak standard load might not have done. To prevent failures to feed on the return stroke, the leaf-type mainspring in the butt was supplemented by an auxiliary return spring within the wooden forestock; the few New Model carbines made omitted this, as they were fitted with stronger coil springs in the butt.

The Parabellum carbines were not especially successful, with only 2,000–3,000 produced, mostly in 1904–05, although stocks lasted until the start of World War I. They did see use by some famous people – the Kaiser used one for hunting, because his withered left arm prevented him from using a bolt-action rifle, while Theodore Roosevelt took another on his arduous 1913 Amazon expedition.

Georg Luger also produced a self-loading rifle prototype in 1906, chambered for the standard 7.92×57mm German rifle round. It used a toggle-action mechanism, but was not related to the pistol and never entered volume production.

Two 7.65mm 'Old Model' carbines. The upper example is an early 1900 variant with a five-position sight mounted on the rear toggle, while the lower version is the more common 1902 variant, with a three-position sight above the chamber. (© Royal Armouries PR.7525 and XII.3585)

Baby Lugers

DWM produced four 'Baby Parabellum' prototypes in 1924–25, two chambered for .32 ACP (7.65mm auto, much less powerful than 7.65mm Parabellum) and two for .380 ACP (9mm Short). All had 75mm barrels, and short five-round (9mm) or six-round (7.65mm) magazines. They differed significantly from standard Parabellums, but retained the recoil-operated toggle-lock design. Aimed at the pocket pistol market, their locked-breech design was both unnecessary for the low-powered cartridges and too expensive to compete with cheap blowback designs. Other 'pocket pistols' were produced by shortening standard guns. A seven-shot

pistol converted from a standard New Model weapon with 80mm barrel and shortened grip was supposedly owned by Georg Luger himself. Mauser also made four 'Pocket Parabellums' in the 1970s (two each of 9mm and 7.65mm) by shortening the barrel and grips of standard 29/70 and 06/73 pistols being produced at the time.

The 7.65mm Furrer M1919 submachine gun (above) was effectively a Luger action mounted in a carbine stock, designed by the head of Waffenfabrik Bern, which produced Swiss military Lugers. The Bergmann MP 18 (below) was not related to the Luger technically, but took over the tactical role of the LP 08. It fed from the same 32-round snail drum, fitted with a slide-on collar to reinforce the neck. (© Royal Armouries PR.10304 and PR.7354)

Full-automatic Lugers

Converting Parabellum pistols to full automatic was straightforward – Luger demonstrated a full-automatic Parabellum as early as 1901, and the Dutch also converted a prototype to full automatic. Both used a simple modified sear bar, similar to the 1914 Navarro conversion, where the closing toggle tripped the sear and fired the next shot. This made them 'all or nothing' weapons – if set to full automatic, they fired until the magazine emptied, though the user could theoretically use the grip safety to stop the weapon firing. Later conversions offered more controllable selective fire, where the weapon continued firing only while the trigger was held down, though the earliest of these (the 1916 Swiss Senn device) required the use of a screwdriver to switch between semi- and full-automatic modes. The light working parts meant a rate of fire around 1,200rd/min, though, and the magazine emptied in ⅓ of a second. Coupled with the light weight of the pistol, this made it very difficult to control on full automatic.

The LP 08 with its stock and drum magazine obviously offered better controllability, and interest in full-automatic versions revived briefly. Even so, while converting an LP 08 into a full-automatic weapon was feasible, it was obviously better to design weapons specifically for the job, such as the Bergmann MP 18. As an odd footnote, the Furrer M1919 submachine gun, developed by Adolf Furrer, the director of Waffenfabrik Bern, was essentially a long-barrelled full-automatic 7.65mm Parabellum action mounted in a Bergmann-style carbine stock. While it functioned, its complexity and cost condemned it to obscurity.

Odd Lugers

Aside from hybrid 'parts guns' made up from whatever old components manufacturers wished to use up, customers could order commercial pistols with a wide range of options such as longer barrels. A 1903 patent also exists for a modified toggle train, which improved the smoothness of the action and reduced the strain on parts. It was more complex to produce and required a redesigned grip safety, however, and never progressed beyond the prototype stage.

Mauser experimented with cast-zinc frames in 1938. These were significantly cheaper than traditional machined frames, but were not strong enough and fractured quickly during testing with 9mm ammunition.

USE
Taking the Luger into battle

OPERATION AND MAINTENANCE

Firing the Luger

Models vary slightly, but the most common – the P 08 – is typical. Starting with the pistol set to 'safe', the user slides a full magazine into the grip until it is locked home. Pulling the toggle grips up and to the rear chambers the first round. The safety catch is at the rear left side of the frame. The P 08 safety is set to 'GESICHERT' ('safe') when in the down position, and pushed up with the thumb to fire.

The raked grip means the weapon points intuitively, making aiming easy. Sights are a simple V-notch at the rear of the frame, and a front blade at the muzzle. The user puts the front sight on the target and centres it in the notch of the rear sight. Trigger pull varies, but can be slightly 'mushy' due to the complex system of levers it actuates. Accuracy is excellent for a pistol, because the barrel and breech recoil in a straight line, rather than dropping as in the Browning system. The moderate recoil is easily controlled, even using the single-handed grip taught to pistol shooters of the period. The toggle pops up briefly into the line of sight after firing, which can be initially disconcerting but in fact has no practical effect – it only begins to rise once the bullet has left the barrel, so there is no effect on accuracy even if the user flinches.

The empty cartridge case is ejected upwards and slightly forwards. The toggle locks to the rear when the last round is fired, giving a clear visible indication as to when the weapon is out of ammunition. To reload, the user depresses the magazine-release button, located at the front of the grip just behind the trigger guard. The empty magazine drops free, allowing the user to insert a replacement and pull the toggle back to chamber the first round.

At the moment of firing (**1**), both barrel and toggle group are in a straight line. When the pistol fires, both barrel and toggle group move backwards together until the toggle drums hit the cam ramps machined into the exterior of the frame (**2**), which causes the toggle to break upwards and open the breech. The toggle continues to fold up and back until the pistol reaches full recoil (**3**), after which the mainspring begins to contract, pulling the toggle down and forward to close the action and chamber the next round. Note that one pistol (**1**) has been depicted with the old-style leaf-type mainspring in the butt, the other (**3**) with the later coil mainspring which replaced it.

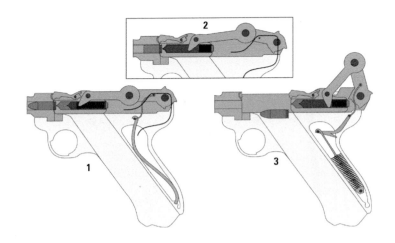

The long-barrelled LP 08 could be used as a pistol, but was best fitted with its flat-board shoulder stock. This allowed a much more stable firing position, with the gun stabilized by shoulder as well as hand. The author was initially unsure where to put his front hand, as there is no forestock and gripping the barrel directly is unwise because it recoils backwards, but using the left hand to cup the right hand on the pistol grip worked reasonably well. The firing position with butt tucked into the shoulder brings the user's eye much closer to the pistol, so the LP 08 rear sight was moved forward and placed atop the chamber, allowing better eye relief. The rear sight has eight positions, rather optimistically calibrated to 800m and adjusted by moving a

The author firing a 7.65mm Swiss Modell 06/29 Luger, in the approved period shooting stance. He found it a very pleasant and accurate pistol to shoot. (Trevor Bain)

Lugers for machine-gun detachments

The German Army adopted machine guns enthusiastically before World War I; each infantry regiment included a six-gun machine-gun company. By 1918, this had increased to three 12-gun companies per infantry regiment. These units were early recipients of the P 08, each being authorized 93 pistols. The first German Army Lugers were bought specifically to equip the experimental detachments in 1907, before the P 08 was adopted, and thus received standard 9mm New Models, some with grip safeties.

Pistols were necessary because machine-gunners (unlike artillerymen) were stationed near the front line, and too heavily burdened with ammunition boxes and water cans to carry rifles.

The German Maxim MG 08 could deliver long-range harassing fire, but many engagements took place at surprisingly close range, because preparatory artillery bombardments invariably targeted known machine-gun positions. The machine-gunners retreated to deep bunkers, emerging immediately after the barrage lifted to engage enemy troops advancing behind it. The MG 08 was dependable and effective, but its heavy sled mount limited the gun's traverse, and crews had to cover the flanks of their position to avoid being overrun. Chances of survival were not good if their position fell; like snipers and flamethrower men, captured machine-gunners were often shot out of hand by vengeful enemy troops.

A German MG 08 machine gun being carried by two of its crew during World War I. The limited traverse permitted by its heavy sled mount meant the crew's holstered pistols were needed to defend the flanks of their position. The leading man carries a hauling line for the gun over his shoulder. (Bettmann/Getty Images)

While P 08 production was stepped up as rapidly as possible, the Army also purchased large numbers of 'substitute pistols'. Meanwhile, rear-echelon units were equipped with the old Reichsrevolver types, blowback pocket pistols or even captured Russian Nagant revolvers.

The popular image of World War I has British and French troops being mown down while assaulting German trench lines, but the German doctrine of invariably counter-attacking immediately to regain lost ground meant they were often the attackers tactically, even when on the strategic defensive. Artillery was by far the greatest killer on the Western Front, and machine guns laid down devastating defensive fires. Neither artillery nor machine guns could go forward with the advancing troops, however, and the main infantry weapons remained the rifle and pistol, increasingly supplemented by the new hand grenades. The close-quarter fighting when clearing or raiding enemy trench lines – or repelling enemy troops attempting the same – made many soldiers appreciate the close-range firepower of a pistol in addition to their rifle and bayonet. This was especially true for the Germans, though their long and unwieldy Gewehr 98 rifle was increasingly replaced with shorter, handier carbines.

Men who could acquire a pistol invariably did so, whether authorized or not – whereas almost one-third of rifles issued to new German soldiers were reissues of weapons recovered from the battlefield, very few pistols were recovered in this manner, because men who found pistols invariably kept or traded them. Trench warfare made the long-barrelled LP 08 pistol

The Germans adopted numerous 'substitute pistols' during World War I, including 150,000 Mauser C96 pistols. The C96 (below) could be easily modified to take the standard 9mm round, and such pistols were marked with a large red '9' on the grip. This marking was also occasionally burned into P 08 grips (above; this example lacks its trigger) from over-zealous application or misunderstanding of the directive, as it served no purpose on Lugers. The pistols illustrated are from the Small Arms School Collection.

Cavalry mêlée on the Eastern Front, August 1914 (opposite)

The battles of Tannenberg and the Masurian Lakes in August and September 1914 removed the immediate Russian threat to East Prussia even though Germany failed to defeat France quickly as the Schlieffen Plan envisaged. Reconnaissance was crucial in the open spaces of the Eastern Front, and with few aircraft available, much of the work fell to cavalry which could operate unconstrained by the trenches and barbed wire of the West. Without radios, however, cavalry scouts could only report what they saw if they were able to return to base, and driving off or killing enemy scouting detachments was also a key cavalry role.

Both sides armed their cavalry to fight on foot if necessary – the Russian Mosin 'Dragoon Rifle' was only 60mm shorter than the standard version, while the German Karabiner 98AZ was short only when compared to the unwieldy Gewehr 98. They were also equipped with lances for shock action, and swords for close-quarter mêlée. A pistol which could be used with one hand while the other controlled the horse was obviously a great asset to a cavalryman issued with it, as a pistol bullet could not be parried and could put an opponent down before he came within sword reach. Once the magazine was empty, though, or if the shooter missed – and being mounted on a frightened horse rarely improves one's accuracy – then the pistol was a poor weapon to parry a sword cut, and some men thus preferred to trust to swords for close work.

The LP 08 at war

The LP 08 was adopted by the German Army in 1913, but it took some time to finalize the details, produce manuals and so on, and the project had relatively low priority. As a result, very few LP 08s were delivered before the outbreak of war in August 1914. Worse, the rapid expansion of the Army put extra pressure on pistol production, and rather than receiving new LP 08s, many artillerymen found themselves stuck with their obsolete revolvers for much of the war.

Meanwhile, personnel of the Army's flying service were armed with the standard P 08. They believed the LP 08 would be more useful, and wished to adopt it to arm all aircrew. Once again, however, few were available by the outbreak of war, and many aircrew who had transferred from other branches such as the cavalry kept their standard P 08s. Accounts from the early days of the war certainly mention aircrew using pistols and carbines against enemy aircraft, but machine guns quickly became the standard armament for air combat as aircraft became more powerful. The flying service limited the issue of LP 08s to pilots, as opposed to other aircrew, in autumn 1916. In December 1917 it trialled a full-automatic LP 08, though one cannot help thinking that more effective weapons were available by that point.

In fact, the main users of the LP 08 would not be airmen or artillerymen, but infantrymen. Although very few LP 08s were available for the first year of the war, the advantages of their high rate of fire at close range had obvious utility for trench raids and so forth.

Meanwhile, the Army was experimenting with fitting high-capacity sheet-metal drum magazines to early self-loading rifles such as the Swiss-made Mondragon. Perfecting self-loading mechanisms capable of handling full-power rifle rounds proved difficult, but the Army realized that the drum-magazine concept could be applied to stocked LP 08 pistols. The result was the 32-round *Trommelmagazin* (drum magazine), which gave the quick-firing LP 08 a significant boost to firepower, and allowed sustained action without the need to carry implausible numbers of eight-round pistol magazines. The value of the LP 08 led to a *Kriegsministerium* (War Department) order of October 1916, which authorized the issue to each infantry company of ten LP 08s and 100 *Trommelmagazin*, over and above their usual complement of pistols. These were to be used to equip combat patrols and to repel enemy assaults, as the War Department believed the drum magazine effectively doubled the pistol's firepower, making it second only to machine guns in terms of the rate of fire (Görtz & Sturgess 2010: 426).

Each LP 08 was also issued with a wooden *Patronenkasten* (ammunition box) containing five drum magazines, five canvas

The German Army's aviation forces used the LP 08 to arm aircrew such as the observer of this Aviatik B.I reconnaissance aircraft, in a posed photograph probably from 1914. It was soon superseded by machine guns, however. (Tom Laemlein/Armor Plate Press)

magazine carriers, 30 16-round boxes of ammunition (480 rounds in total) and a magazine-filler tool to ease the difficult job of loading rounds into the drums. Orders were placed for another 200,000 LP 08 pistols and 1,000,000 drum magazines at the beginning of November 1916, but would obviously take some time to deliver.

At the very end of the war, the German Army introduced the Bergmann Maschinenpistole 18 (MP 18), the first practical submachine gun. This used the same 9mm rounds and drum magazine as the LP 08, inserted into the side of the weapon rather than into the pistol grip. Although larger, the MP 18 had the same 200mm barrel length as the LP 08, and thus almost identical performance. Importantly, though, it was designed for full-automatic fire from the start, using a simple blowback design with

a relatively heavy bolt that kept the rate of fire down to 500rd/min. The weapon was thus reasonably controllable, especially given its greater (4.2kg) weight. Significantly, the Germans termed the new weapon a 'machine pistol' – the tactical instructions for the new MP 18 were identical to those for the LP 08, and it was intended for the same role.

Though well-known today, few MP 18s actually reached the troops. By contrast, the LP 08 seems to have made a considerable impact, because the International Control Commission supervising the post-Versailles German Army specifically prohibited the Reichswehr from having stocked pistols. Most examples were destroyed, though some were given new short barrels to convert them into standard P 08s.

An LP 08 (above) and magazines (below) from the Small Arms School Collection. The LP 08 was initially issued with three eight-round magazines and a shoulder stock, but was greatly enhanced when the 32-round *Trommelmagazin* (drum magazine) became available later. The stock buckled to the rear of the leather holster, and both were carried on a shoulder strap, though versions with belt fittings exist. Note the folding winding lever visible on the detached drum.

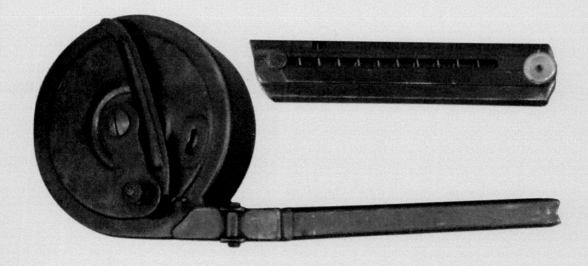

The Germans used airborne forces very successfully on a small scale during the early Blitzkrieg campaigns in Europe and during the invasion of mainland Greece. In May 1941, they launched a much larger airborne operation – *Unternehmen Merkur* (Operation *Mercury*), the invasion of Crete. The German plan was for *Fallschirmjäger* to seize the airfield at Maleme and the smaller airstrips at Heraklion and Rethymno, which would then be used to land follow-on forces, along with reinforcements delivered by amphibious landings. Aided by signal intercepts, the Allied defenders had correctly anticipated the main German objectives, and were able to hold the airfield and inflict heavy casualties on the airborne troops. Landing with their weapons in separate containers, the lightly armed German paratroopers found themselves at a serious disadvantage, and took heavy casualties very quickly. Many of the survivors were pinned down by Allied fire and unable to recover their weapons or organize themselves. Several were even beaten to death by Cretan civilians before they could disentangle themselves from their parachutes.

Here, three *Fallschirmjäger* shelter from Allied rifle fire; a fourth has become a casualty while trying to retrieve one of the containers holding their weapons, which has landed in open ground. The rifleman nearest the viewer holds his P 08 while calling the rest of his section together; paratroopers jumping from the same aircraft typically landed in a rough line 50–100m apart. The middle man has a Walther P 38, unusual but not unknown at this point in the war. The third man fires an MP 40 submachine gun; this was compact enough to be carried beneath the parachute harness with the stock folded, but only one *Fallschirmjäger* in four was issued with one, due to the weapon's short effective range. All three men still wear the protective kneepads – and in the case of the MP 40-armed man, the protective gloves – issued to prevent injury during rough landings. They have taken off their long jump smocks, which covered their equipment harnesses during the jump, and put their smocks back on again with the equipment worn on the outside, to allow easier access to weapons and ammunition.

LUGERS AFTER 1945

World War II ended with Western Europe liberated, but with its armed forces eliminated by Nazi occupation or dependent on weapons supplied by the victorious Allies, which would not continue indefinitely.

France

France was theoretically among the 'victorious' powers, but her pre-war armaments had been seized during the occupation, and German troops in France surrendered their weapons to US or British forces, rather than French ones. Meanwhile, the small 'Free French' forces were largely equipped with US weapons provided as military aid. Bringing pre-war French designs back into production was unrealistic, because they were long outdated even if the tooling remained. French forces therefore needed a short-term source of weapons while newer French-designed weapons were developed and produced.

Germany had been divided into four occupation zones by the Allied Powers, and fortuitously the almost-intact Mauser plant at Oberndorf was in the French zone. This was put back into operation to produce weapons for the French Army. Most were Kar 98k rifles (48,000) and P 38 pistols (35,000), but the plant also held stocks of P 08 parts pre-dating the switch to P 38 production. Some of these were assembled into Lugers for presentation to Allied officers or sale to US soldiers as souvenirs, including a few 'Artillery Models' using legacy barrels and sights transferred from DWM to Mauser before the war, along with the

The Luger as battlefield souvenir

Allied soldiers favoured Lugers as souvenirs, while British troops often preferred them to their own pistols, in both world wars. When World War I infantry officer Charles Carrington found a dead German officer, he took his pistol, believing it to be superior to the Webley he and his colleagues carried (Carrington 1991: 195). David Render, who served as a tank commander in the British Army almost 30 years later, recalled that it had been a particular ambition of his to obtain a Luger; he praised its smooth action and believed it was a better pistol than the Enfield revolver (Render 2016: 138). This 'souvenir hunting' did not end when the fighting did. In Berlin during 1945, British tanker Bill Bellamy recalled one US serviceman showing off a Luger he had bought for 100 cigarettes from a Soviet soldier (Bellamy 2005: 219).

Although the United States never adopted the Luger – despite coming very close to doing so – this World War I US Army soldier has managed to acquire one as a souvenir. (Tom Laemlein/Armor Plate Press)

Lugers were popular souvenirs among Allied military personnel, and might be purchased or traded as well as captured personally. Here a lieutenant of the US 9th Air Force inspects a captured German Luger pistol at a base in France in January 1945. An M1 carbine hangs on the wall behind him. The US Army issued these light semi-automatic weapons from 1942 to arm men whose duties prevented them carrying a full-sized rifle, and who might have been issued pistols in other armies. The carbine offered better range and accuracy than a pistol, and folding-stock versions were issued to many paratroopers. The selective-fire M2 version which appeared in October 1944 meant it could also replace the submachine gun. (Photo12/UIG/Getty Images)

'better' pistol than the Luger, though having fired both, the author subjectively preferred the Luger due to its better ergonomics. Even so, range shooting is different from carrying a pistol every day, where the Walther was strongest. In the author's opinion, the Colt 1911 was probably the best of the pistols assessed here, and certainly his personal preference. It shared the Luger's advantages of natural pointability and quick reloading, but had two key advantages – a big, heavy cartridge that left nobody in doubt about its stopping power, and John Browning's simple, rugged dropping-link action. It carried one round less in its magazine, and was somewhat bigger than the Luger. Overall, though, it was a superior weapon that remained in US service until 1986.

TECHNICAL IMPACT

The Luger had a profound impact upon pistol design. The advantages of placing the magazine in the grip seem obvious in retrospect, but many early pistol designs followed revolver lines and placed it before the grip. Some even did this after the Luger appeared, and were outcompeted by weapons following Luger's lead. Equally, the detachable box magazine seems so simple, and has become so universal, that we forget it was a radical innovation when introduced and that the Luger's initial competitors loaded from chargers, rather than magazines. Even so, it was the 9mm Parabellum (9×19mm) round for the P 08 that would be the Luger's most lasting influence.

Luger magazines

The detachable box magazine was one of the most important innovations in the Borchardt and Luger designs, setting them apart from other early semi-automatic pistols, which loaded from rifle-style chargers. The Luger magazine was a complex and relatively expensive feature, however – each cost 2.5 Marks, so the pair supplied with each P 08 made up 10 per cent of the weapon's total cost. Magazines were interchangeable between pistols, but those supplied with each pistol were numbered to it, like other small parts. Each P 08 was issued with a single spare magazine, carried on the holster spine. P 04s and LP 08s were issued with two spare magazines each, carried in a separate two-cell leather magazine pouch.

Early magazines were assembled from seven parts including two stamped-steel sides and a machined walnut base with dished roundels on the bottom. These served as finger grips, and made it obvious the pistol had a magazine in it, for safety reasons. The feed lips were reshaped slightly with the change to the New Model, to handle straight-sided 9mm bullets better. The wooden magazine bases were replaced with aluminium ones from 1925, then black plastic ones during World War II, to conserve strategic materials. Existing magazines continued in service on both occasions, however. German magazine bodies were originally nickel-plated, though late World War I magazines were blued instead, or even plain steel. Magazines reverted to nickel in the 1920s, until Mauser reintroduced a blued finish in 1936–37.

A stronger and more reliable Haenel magazine (often incorrectly referred to as the 'extruded' or 'monolithic' type) replaced the original from 1935 for the police, and from 1939 for the armed forces. Rather than being crimped from two separate halves, this was stamped from a single sheet, folded to shape around a metal die and welded along the rear seam, which was then polished smooth.

DATES	DWM (GERMAN P 08 AND LP 08)	MAUSER (GERMAN P 08)	ERFURT (P 08 AND LP 08)	OTHER	TOTAL
1900–19				131,136 (DWM: foreign contracts and commercial production)	131,136
1906–16				40,000 (DWM: P 04 production)	40,000
1906–11	60,520		10,000		70,520
1912	10,000		21,000		31,000
1913	26,050		23,000		49,050
1914	40,300		30,000		70,300
1915	136,500				136,500
1916	183,000		75,000		258,000
1917	173,000		190,000		363,000
1918	118,000		160,000		278,000
1919–30				204,248 (DWM: foreign, police and commercial production)	204,248
1921–22				6,000 (Vickers: KNIL contract)	6,000
1918–33				17,873 (W + F Bern: Modell 1900/06)	17,873
1925–34				12,000 (Simson: military production)	12,000
1934		11,000			11,000
1935		54,000			54,000
1936		89,500			89,500
1937		126,000			126,000
1938		114,000			114,000
1939		123,500			123,500
1940		137,000			137,000
1941		145,000			145,000
1942		110,000			110,000
1933–46				29,858 (W + F Bern: Modell 06/29)	29,858
1935–45				14,500 (Krieghoff: Luftwaffe and commercial production)	14,500
1935–43				50,000 (Mauser: commercial, export, police and forestry service production)	50,000
1945–46				3,500 (Mauser: French production)	3,500
TOTAL	747,370	910,000	509,000	509,115	2,675,485

markings on the safety catch and extractor (see page 17). They were distributed by DWM's US agent, Hans Tauscher of New York, who felt 'Luger' was a better name than 'Parabellum' and always referred to the pistol as such, popularizing the name in the English-speaking world. Colt and Browning brought a lawsuit to prevent the Parabellum's sale in the United States, alleging it infringed Browning's 1897 patent on recoil-operated pistols. The US courts unsurprisingly found against them, because if a patent was understood to cover any weapon operated by

The Brazilian 'Cangaceiro' (bandit) Chico Pereira with a privately purchased Luger 'Artillery' in 9mm, *c.*1925. (Courtesy Rostand Medeiros)

recoil (as it had to be, to cover the Luger) then Browning himself would be in breach of Maxim's earlier patent on recoil operation.

Tauscher had retained his original German nationality, and his business was confiscated when the United States entered World War I in 1917. In 1922, the US government granted the US rights to the Luger patents to H.J. Panzer & Co., who came to an agreement with A.F. Stoeger & Co., DWM's preferred licensee. Stoeger registered 'Parabellum' and 'Luger' as trademarks in the United States, which would lead to an interesting situation later. Most Lugers imported by Stoeger carried his branding, though some companies such as Abercrombie & Fitch imported guns directly.

Highly decorated pistols, often with matching cases, were given as 'presentation pieces' to high-ranking military officers and political leaders in the hope of generating future sales. These often featured elaborate engraving, gold plating and inlays of ivory. None of the manufacturers did such work in house, instead sending the guns out for decoration after manufacture. (© Royal Armouries XII.11476)

Many wartime commercial pistols used parts which failed rigorous military quality controls but were still serviceable, while commercial pistols sold immediately after World War I often contained military parts, or were refurbished ex-military weapons. Parabellums produced in Germany in the early 1920s were restricted to 7.65mm calibre and barrels of 100mm or less (usually 90mm, 95mm or 98mm) by the Versailles Treaty, though some were rebarrelled abroad. Sales declined severely in the 1930s, both because of the 1929 Great Depression and the appearance of both the Colt 1911 and more modern 9mm pistols. After World War II, the handgun market was flooded with captured 'war trophy' Lugers, often at low prices.

The Luger is revived

Aside from 'bring-back' guns which came home with returning servicemen, thousands of war-surplus Lugers were imported into the United States after World War II, notably by the Interarms company run by Sam Cummings. He purchased large numbers of surplus weapons cheaply in Europe immediately after the war, from cash-strapped governments happy to receive money for weapons they would otherwise have destroyed or dumped at sea. These guns were refurbished in Britain before being shipped to the United States where they were sold at very competitive prices by mail order. Lobbying from US gun companies (who could not compete against these cheap imports) and concerns over the easy availability of guns to criminals led to the 1968 Gun Control Act, however. This made import of war-surplus foreign weapons much more difficult, though in practice the supply of cheap wartime guns was running out by then anyway. The 1968 Act only applied to 'war surplus' weapons, not newly produced ones, and Interarms persuaded Mauser to resume production of the Luger in 1967, for commercial sale in the United States.

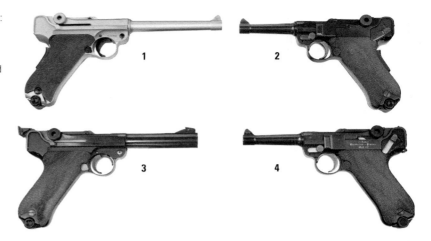

Four revived Mauser Parabellums: a 150mm-barrel version with a satin finish (**1**); the basic model produced for Interarms (**2**); a heavy-barrel target model (**3**); and a '75th Anniversary' P 08 commemorative (**4**). (© Royal Armouries PR.12887, PR.12885, PR.12888 and PR.13520)

Mauser initially believed that resuming production would be reasonably straightforward, because the company still possessed the original production blueprints for the P 08. These did not meet 1960s standards, however, and would need to be expensively redrawn. As an alternative, Mauser approached Waffenfabrik Bern, which produced the Swiss Modell 06/29 Luger until 1947. For DM 259,000 (about $60,000), Mauser received complete blueprint packages, tooling, jigs and gauges, although these were not always directly usable. Mauser began production of new 7.65mm and 9mm pistols from 1969. The new Mauser pistols were effectively copies of the Swiss Modell 06/29, however. This made sense from Mauser's point of view, because the Swiss changes simplified production and made the weapon more cost-effective. Cummings was adamant, though, that his customers wanted the iconic German Luger. Interarms eventually agreed to take the initial Swiss-style pistols (known as the Modell 29/70) provided Mauser modified the design so future deliveries looked more like P 08s. Obviously, changing an existing production line involved costs for Mauser, both directly and in lost production, but they had little alternative. Even so, the resulting guns were not completely identical to the P 08, resembling a New Model with grip safety and no stock lug. They appeared in late 1971, and were known as the Modell 06/73.

Although the Modell 06/73 sold reasonably well, it was never the commercial success either party hoped for, and Mauser ceased production of new pistols in 1986. The company continued to assemble pistols from existing components until 1998, however. As a marketing ploy, these were targeted at the collector's market in a series of limited 'commemorative' editions of only 250 weapons each, copying desirable historical Lugers such as the 'Artillery Model' or the US 'Cartridge Counter' model, with the base pistol modified using custom-made barrels, sights and other components and engraved appropriately.

Mauser considered producing a .45 ACP version, but only two prototypes were produced.

In 2006, Krieghoff produced exact copies of the P 08, using modern five-axis CNC machines. These copies were well made, but very expensive at more than €10,500/$8,000 each and only 200 were produced.

ERMA and Stoeger 'Lugers'

Erfurter Maschinenfabrik (ERMA) produced several sub-calibre training units for the Luger before World War II, but after 1945 the plant was in the Soviet occupation zone. The company was reconstituted in the West, and produced a blowback .22 LR target pistol (the EP 22) in 1964. This strongly resembled the Parabellum, using the toggle system developed for the earlier conversion kit. A second model, the KGP 68, appeared in 1968. This resembled an improved EP 22, but chambered 7.65mm ACP or .380 ACP cartridges, with the toggle system modified to a delayed-blowback system. The KGP 68 was followed by the KGP 69, essentially an updated and improved EP 22. Although often referred to as 'ERMA Lugers', and despite the strong visual resemblance, these guns also do not form part of the Luger family.

The revived Mauser/Interarms pistols legally had to be referred to as 'Parabellums', because 'Luger' was registered as a US trademark in the 1930s by DWM's US importer, A.F. Stoeger & Co. From 1969 to 1985, Stoeger marketed its own .22 LR pistols under the Luger branding, in both standard and target pistol configurations. Although these guns had a strong (and entirely intentional) visual resemblance to the famous P 08, they were simple blowback designs without a locked breech. Despite the branding and visual resemblance, though, they cannot be considered 'Lugers' in any real sense.

Two versions of the ERMA 4mm sub-calibre trainers produced to allow cheap practice without the need for a full-sized firing range, one in its wooden case and the other installed on a P 08. (© Royal Armouries PR.12890 and PR.10773)

ERMA Luger lookalikes – from the top, a KGP 68 in 7.65mm Short (**1**), a KGP 68A in 9mm Short (**2**) and an EP 22 in .22 LR (**3**). (© Royal Armouries PR.4135, PR.12648 and PR.10474)

A Stoeger .22 LR 'Luger'. Despite the strong and intentional physical resemblance, these blowback designs were only suitable for light cartridges. (© Royal Armouries PR.7855)

CONCLUSION

The Luger was a ground-breaking weapon when it appeared. Its stand-out quality of design is evident when compared to that of its immediate contemporaries such as the Mauser, Mannlicher and Roth, which quickly fell by the wayside. By contrast, the Luger was widely adopted, and generally well regarded by users. It served successfully through both world wars, and was ultimately replaced not by something offering better performance, but by something which could be manufactured more cheaply – the Luger was a product of its time, dependent on high-quality machining and craftsmanship, and did not suit a world in which weapons were mass-produced from sheet-metal stampings. Its toggle-action mechanism was strong and effective, but expensive to produce – strikingly, while Spanish and Chinese workshops produced innumerable cheap Mauser 'Broomhandle' copies, they never copied the Luger – and not used on later pistols, with manufacturers preferring the simpler Browning-designed dropping-link mechanism despite its theoretically slightly poorer accuracy. Even so, the Luger had a lasting impact on pistol design. Its overall configuration, with the detachable box magazine placed in the grip, was followed by almost all subsequent pistols.

Battlefields are generally dominated by long guns, and most pistols were only used for close-range personal defence. The Luger was a rare exception to this, because the stocked LP 08 effectively gave birth to an entirely new class of weapon, the submachine gun. Perhaps the Luger's most important legacy, though, was its ammunition. The 9mm Parabellum (9×19mm) round became the standard NATO pistol round, and has dominated Western submachine-gun and pistol design ever since.

The Luger's success, combined with frequent film and television appearances, made it one of the most recognizable pistols of the 20th century. It may have been surpassed technically by modern high-capacity semi-automatics, but surviving examples can still match them for accuracy. It remains almost the only wartime weapon actually put back into production – a fitting tribute to what must be judged one of the most important handguns ever produced.

OPPOSITE

A *Gefreiter* (corporal) armed with a P 08 pistol during the fighting for Kerch, in the Crimea, during World War II. He has a stick grenade tucked behind his pistol holster, and spare ammunition for his squad's MG 34 machine gun draped round his neck. (Tom Laemlein/Armor Plate Press)

76

BIBLIOGRAPHY

Baudino. Mauro & van Vlimmeren, Gerben (2010). *The Parabellum is Back! 1945–2000*. Galesburg, IL: Brad Simpson Publishing.

Baum, John (2007). *Firearm 98 and Pistol 08*. Lisbon, OH: Self-published. Translation of German manual.

Bellamy, Bill (2005). *Troop Leader: A Tank Commander's Story*. Stroud: Sutton Publishing.

Carrington, Charles (1991). *Soldier from the Wars Returning*. Aldershot: Gregg Revivals. Originally published in 1965.

Clifford, Dorrien (2016). 'The First Victims of the Great War: A Further Look at the Joncherey Incident – Before and After', in *Stand To!* No. 105: 27–33.

Datig, Fred A. (1955). *The Luger Pistol (Pistole Parabellum): Its History & Development from 1893–1945*. Los Angeles, CA: Borden Publishing.

Datig, Fred A. (1992). *Luger – Monograph IV: The Swiss Variations 1897–1947*. Los Angeles, CA: FADCO Publishing.

Gibson, Randall (1980). *The Krieghoff Parabellum*. Midland, TX: Centenary Publications.

Görtz, Joachim & Sturgess, Geoffrey L. (2010). *Pistole Parabellum: The History of the 'Luger System'*. Three volumes. Cobourg: Collector Grade Publications.

Görtz, Joachim & Walter, John (1988). *The Navy Luger: The 9mm Pistole 1904 and the Imperial German Navy: A Concise Illustrated History*. Eastbourne: Lyon Publishing International.

Hogg, Ian V. (1971). *German Pistols and Revolvers 1871–1945*. Harrisburg, PA: Stackpole Books.

Hogg, Ian V. (2001). *German Handguns: The Complete Book of the Pistols and Revolvers of Germany, 1869 to the Present*. London: Greenhill Books.

Jones, H.E. (1959). *Luger Variations*. Los Angeles, CA: Southern Press.

Kenyon, Jr, Charles (1991). *Luger: The Multi-National Pistol*. Moline, IL, Richard Ellis Publications.

Kenyon, Jr, Charles (2008). *Lugers at Random*. Cincinnati, OH: CJA Publications. Originally published in 1969.

Lubbeck, William (2010). *At Leningrad's Gates: The Story of a Soldier with Army Group North*. Newbury: Casemate.

Martens, Bas J. & de Vries, Guus (1994). *The Dutch Luger (Parabellum) – A Complete History*. Alexandria, VA: Ironside International Publishers.

Martens, Bas J. & de Vries, Guus (2002). *The P08 Luger Pistol*. Oosterbeek: Special Interest Publications BV.

McFarland, J. Davis (1986). *The P08 Parabellum Luger Automatic Pistol*. El Dorado, AR: Desert Publications. Translated from several German pamphlets.

Render, David & Tootal, Stuart (2016). *Tank Action: An Armoured Troop Commander's War 1944–45*. London: Weidenfeld & Nicolson.

Sayre, Edward C. (2010). *The Luger Snail Drum and Other Accessories for the Artillery Model Luger*. Woonsocket, RI: Mowbray Publishers.

Skennerton, Ian (2004). *9mm Luger P08 Pistol Handbook*. Philadelphia, PA: Ray Riling Arms Books.

Walter, John (1977). *Luger: An Illustrated History of the Handguns of Hugo Borchardt and Georg Luger, 1875 to the present day*. London: Arms & Armour Press

Walter, John (1980). *German Military Handguns, 1879–1918*. London: Arms & Armour Press.

Walter, John (1986). *The Luger Book: The Encyclopedia of the Borchardt and Borchardt-Luger handguns, 1885–1985*. London: Arms & Armour Press.

Walter, John (2001). *The Luger Story: The Standard History of the World's Most Famous Handgun*. London: Greenhill Books. Originally published in 1995.

Walter, John (2004). *Guns of the Third Reich*. London: Greenhill Books.

A German officer directs troops near Kerch in the Crimea during 1942. Although production of the Luger ended in September that year, it remained in German military service until the end of World War II. (Mondadori Portfolio via Getty Images)

INDEX